This Journal Belongs to:

....

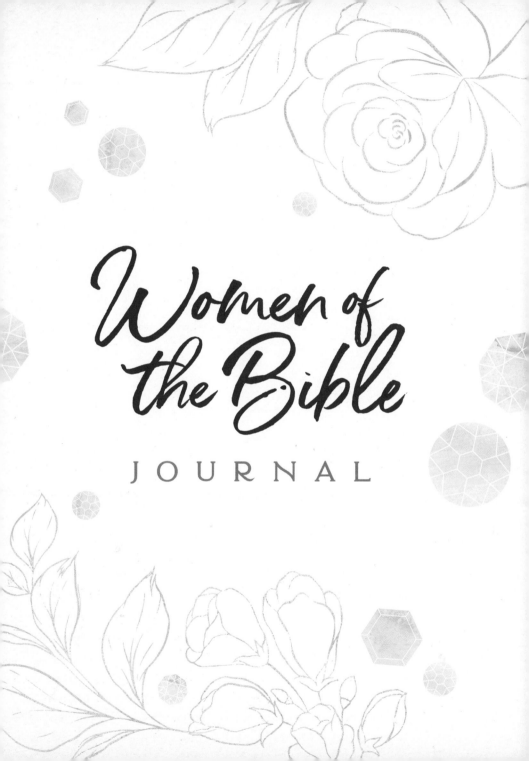

Women of the Bible

JOURNAL

Women of the Bible

JOURNAL

Featuring Fascinating
Study Notes on Each Page

BARBOUR
PUBLISHING

ISBN 978-1-63609-072-6

All scripture quotations, unless otherwise noted, are taken from the King James Version of the Bible.

Scripture quotations marked NIV are taken from the HOLY BIBLE, NEW INTERNATIONAL VERSION®. NIV®. Copyright © 1973, 1978, 1984, 2011 by Biblica, Inc.™ Used by permission. All rights reserved worldwide.

Cover Design: Greg Jackson, Thinkpen Design

Published by Barbour Publishing, Inc., 1810 Barbour Drive, Uhrichsville, Ohio 44683, www.barbourbooks.com

Our mission is to inspire the world with the life-changing message of the Bible.

Member of the
Evangelical Christian
Publishers Association

Printed in China.

YOU WANT THE MOST FROM YOUR TIME IN GOD'S WORD...

this Women of the Bible Journal *provides both interesting study notes and ample space for you to jot down your reflections.*

While the events described in the Bible occurred within a patriarchal social system, the women of scripture have a strong presence. They are remembered for their significant contributions, good and bad:

- Eve, who birthed the human race
- Sarah, matriarch of God's chosen people
- Deborah, who led the Israelite nation
- Delilah, conqueror of Samson
- Mary, mother of God's Son
- Herodias, nemesis of John the Baptist
- Lydia, first European convert to Christianity
- Priscilla, early Christian missionary

Women of the Bible provide both positive and negative examples for us in the twenty-first century. And this journal, featuring fascinating details on scores of these individuals, allows you to capture your own thoughts and feelings as you study. The *Women of the Bible Journal* will become a treasured record of your own walk with God.

Of the approximately 3,400 people named in scripture, around 160 are women. There are about 140 different names of women in the Bible.

Lydia (Acts 16) was a
merchant of purple cloth
in the city of Philippi.
She became a Christian,
was baptized, and
showed hospitality to
the apostle Paul.

When her master contracted leprosy, an unnamed servant girl of the Aramean commander Naaman suggested he go to Elisha the prophet to seek healing. He listened to the girl and was ultimately cleansed after washing seven times in the Jordan River (2 Kings 5).

Lois was a Jewish believer who was mother to Eunice and grandmother to Timothy (2 Timothy 1:5).

Sister to Mary and Lazarus, Martha is characterized as one who kept her household well. At times, though, she was so distracted by serving that she missed out on enjoying Jesus' presence (Luke 10).

Obeying God rather than Pharaoh, Shiphrah, as a midwife to the Hebrews, refused to kill the male babies that were born as she had been ordered to do (Exodus 1).

The "Proverbs 31 woman" was described by a King Lemuel. Some speculate that's a name for Solomon or perhaps Hezekiah.

Abiah, Abihail, Abijah, Aholibamah, and Athaliah were names used by both men and women.

Sarah, wife of the patriarch Abraham, gave birth to their son Isaac at age ninety (Genesis 17:17). No wonder their son's name means "laughter."

Jesus took care of His mother, Mary, from the cross, telling an unnamed disciple (believed to be John), "Here is your mother." (John 19:25–27 NIV). From that point on, the disciple cared for Mary in his home.

Zillah was mother
to Tubal-cain, who
is credited with
inventing metalworking
(Genesis 4:22).

Merab, whose name means "increase" or "multiplication," was the name of King Saul's oldest daughter (1 Samuel 14:49).

Jesus commanded, "Remember Lot's wife" (Luke 17:32). She succumbed to the temptation to look back on the destruction of Sodom and lost her life, becoming a pillar of salt (Genesis 19).

Though we don't know
her name, we know that
the apostle Peter had a
wife, because Jesus healed
Peter's mother-in-law of
a fever (Mark 1:30), and
the apostle Paul asked,
"Don't we have the right to
take a believing wife along
with us, as do the other
apostles and the Lord's
brothers and Cephas?"
(1 Corinthians 9:5 NIV).
Cephas was the name
Jesus gave to Peter
in John 1:42.

Two Old Testament
women were called
Abigail. The name means
"a father's joy."

When the prophet Ezekiel's wife died, he did not mourn publicly. He was obeying God's command, making a point to the sinful Israelites (Ezekiel 24).

Esau's marriage to Judith, a Hittite, caused his parents sorrow. As scripture never mentions her again, the grief she caused her in-laws is our entire legacy of her (Genesis 26:34–35).

Jedidah was wife of Judah's wicked King Amon, who was murdered by his servants. She was mother to Josiah, who became king at the age of eight and ruled well through his life (2 Kings 21:19–22:1).

Ephah, Gomer,
Joanna, and Noah were
names used by both
men and women.

Due to mistreatment
by her mistress, Sarah,
Hagar ran away into the
desert. In her sorrow, she
cried out to God, whom
she named "Thou God
seest me." He was faithful
to meet her in her need
(Genesis 16).

Euodias worked alongside the apostle Paul in the cause of the Gospel. Paul urged Euodias and another woman, Syntyche, to put aside their differences so that the work of the Lord would not be hindered (Philippians 4:2–3).

Mary Magdalene,
one of Jesus' closest
female companions,
had had seven demons
cast out of her by the
Lord (Mark 16:9).

There are at least a half dozen Marys in the New Testament: Jesus' mother; Mary Magdalene; the sister of Martha and Lazarus; the mother of James and Joses who observed the crucifixion (who may also be the wife of Cleophas); the mother of John Mark; and a Roman Christian greeted by the apostle Paul.

The young Jewish woman Esther, cousin of Mordecai, was chosen to become queen of Persia. She was also known as Hadassah (Esther 2:7), meaning "myrtle," a biblical symbol of God's blessing and peace.

Widows, and rules relating to them, are mentioned more than eighty times in scripture.

Adah was one of at least three wives of Esau. She gave birth to their son, Eliphaz (Genesis 36:10).

Gomer, wife of the prophet Hosea, lived a life of prostitution, yet he repeatedly returned to her. His redemption is a picture of God's forgiveness and love (Hosea 2:23).

Ruth, name of the heroine of the Old Testament book by that name, means "companion" or "friend."

An unnamed nurse of Mephibosheth, King Saul's son, heard of impending danger, picked up the boy, and ran. But she dropped him, causing lifelong disability (2 Samuel 4:4).

Tryphena and Tryphosa, two women the apostle Paul credited for their work for the Lord (Romans 16:12), were most likely related and of the same Roman family.

Elisabeth, an older woman who miraculously conceived and gave birth to John the Baptist, was related to Jesus' mother, Mary (Luke 1:26–37).

King Saul gave his daughter Michal to David as his wife. Early in their marriage, she protected her husband against her father's plans to kill him, helping him down through a window to escape (1 Samuel 19).

Adam called his wife
Eve, since she was
"the mother of all living"
(Genesis 3:20). She is only
mentioned by name four
times in the Bible.

2 John is addressed to "the elect lady and her children" (2 John 1:1). Some suggest this "lady" is actually a local church congregation.

Jecholiah, whose name means "powerful," was wife of King Amaziah of Judah and mother of King Azariah, also known as Uzziah (2 Kings 15:1–2).

According to the
Proverbs, a man who
finds a wife has found
"a good thing" and
obtains the "favour
of the LORD"
(Proverbs 18:22).

Zibiah was the mother of Joash, who became king of Judah at age seven. For many years, he "did that which was right in the sight of the LORD" (2 Kings 12:2), which suggests that Zibiah raised him well.

Miriam, sister of Moses and Aaron, was a prophetess of Israel. But when she complained about Moses' wife, she was struck with leprosy. Moses prayed, and God healed her (Numbers 12).

The death of an
unnamed twelve-year-
old girl broke her family's
heart. . .but Jesus turned
their mourning into
dancing by resurrecting
this daughter of Jairus
(Mark 5, Luke 8).

When the pregnant daughter-in-law of the priest Eli learned the ark of the covenant had been captured, her grief sent her into labor. She gave birth to a boy she called Ichabod ("no glory"), then died (1 Samuel 4).

Athaliah was the only ruling queen of Israel or Judah. She reigned over Judah after her son Ahaziah was assassinated by Jehu, future king of Israel. Athaliah then ordered the killing of the rest of Judah's royal family to solidify her claim to the throne. One baby, however, was spirited away by Ahaziah's sister. Six years later, he was proclaimed king and Athaliah was executed (2 Kings 11).

Jesus broke barriers of both ethnicity and sex by talking with a Samaritan woman at the well of Sychar (John 4). Both she and Jesus' disciples were surprised . . .but the Lord used the experience to draw many Samaritans to Himself.

The mother of Jabez
said she gave birth to
him in pain (1 Chronicles
4:9–10). His name
means "sorrowful."

Maachah, Puah,
Shelomith, and Timna
were names used by both
men and women.

Pharaoh honored the once Jewish slave Joseph by giving him a new name, a new position, and a bride, Asenath. She became mother to Manasseh and Ephraim, who headed tribes of Israel (Genesis 41).

Tamar was a beautiful daughter of King David. Her half brother Amnon became obsessed with her and forced himself on her. When Tamar's full brother Absalom heard of the attack, he plotted Amnon's death (2 Samuel 13).

Priscilla, along with her
husband, Aquila, worked
to serve the early church.
Like the apostle Paul,
she was a maker of tents
(Acts 18:1–3).

Hammoleketh was
a granddaughter of
Joseph's son Manasseh
(1 Chronicles 7:14–18).
Her name means "the
queen" or "the regent."

Solomon, credited as the wisest man ever, had seven hundred wives and three hundred concubines (1 Kings 11:3). Sadly, since many of them worshipped idols, he put himself on a path to ruin.

Reumah is the first concubine mentioned in the Bible. She bore four sons to Abraham's brother Nahor (Genesis 22:23–24).

God miraculously
provided children for
at least a half dozen
Bible women, including
Sarah, Rebekah, Rachel,
Manoah's wife, the well-
to-do woman of Shunem,
and Elisabeth.

A foolish decision to support her husband's lie brought death upon an early Christian named Sapphira. She and Ananias conspired to impress the church with an offering they made, indicating they were giving the entire amount of a land sale when, in fact, they had kept back some for themselves (Acts 5).

Deborah was the only female judge (or deliverer) of Israel. She held court under a palm tree but was also a brave warrior who accompanied troops into battle (Judges 4–5).

Huldah was a prophetess in the time of King Josiah. She was consulted when Josiah's officials found the long-forgotten "book of the law" (2 Kings 22).

Elisabeth was six months pregnant with John the Baptist when the angel Gabriel announced to the virgin Mary that she would give birth to Jesus (Luke 1:26–38).

Zeruah was the widowed mother of Jeroboam, an official of King Solomon (1 Kings 11:26). Jeroboam would ultimately lead the northern tribes of Israel to become their own kingdom in opposition to the southern nation of Judah.

Peter's mother-in-law, sick with a fever, was healed by Jesus. She immediately got up from her bed to serve Him (Matthew 8:14–15).

When Lydia accepted the apostle Paul's Gospel invitation along the riverbank near Philippi, she became the first Christian on the European continent (Acts 16).

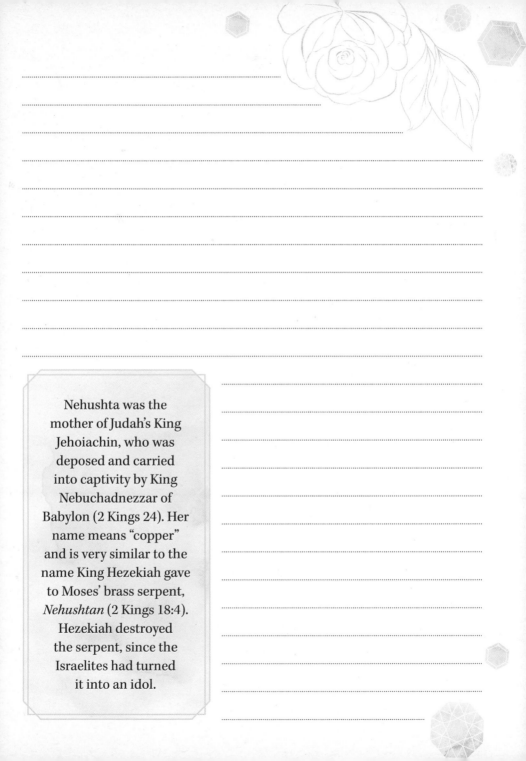

Nehushta was the mother of Judah's King Jehoiachin, who was deposed and carried into captivity by King Nebuchadnezzar of Babylon (2 Kings 24). Her name means "copper" and is very similar to the name King Hezekiah gave to Moses' brass serpent, *Nehushtan* (2 Kings 18:4). Hezekiah destroyed the serpent, since the Israelites had turned it into an idol.

The name of Euodias,
a coworker with
Paul who needed the
apostle's urging to get
along with another
churchwoman, Syntyche,
means "fine traveling"
(Philippians 4:2–3).

Tirzah was a daughter of Zelophehad, an Israelite who died during the wilderness wanderings. She and her sisters asked Moses if they could inherit their father's property in the Promised Land, since Zelophehad had no sons. God answered yes (Numbers 27).

Six Old Testament women were named Maachah. One was a granddaughter of King David who became the favored wife of David's grandson King Rehoboam (2 Chronicles 11:21).

Adam called Eve "Woman, because she was taken out of Man" (Genesis 2:23). Though God had created Adam from the dust of the earth, Eve was made from one of the man's ribs (verse 21).

Noah's wife is mentioned
five times in the flood
account of Genesis, but
she is never quoted. The
unnamed woman was
mother of three sons,
Shem, Ham, and Japheth,
who repopulated the
earth after the deluge
(Genesis 6–9).

A desperate mother of Syrian Phoenicia demonstrated the value of persistence in prayer. She begged Jesus to drive a demon from her daughter, only to hear Him say His ministry was purely to Jews: "First let the children eat all they want," he told her, "for it is not right to take the children's bread and toss it to the dogs." Her response ("Lord," she replied, "even the dogs under the table eat the children's crumbs.") pleased Jesus so much that He granted her request (Mark 7:25–30 NIV).

In an alphabetical list
of women in the King
James Bible, Abi is first.
She was the mother
of Judah's good King
Hezekiah (2 Kings 18:1–2).

In an alphabetical list of women in the King James Bible, Zipporah is last. She was the wife of Moses (Exodus 2).

What kind of mother was Herodias? The kind who would tell her young daughter, whose dance had pleased her stepfather Herod, to request "John Baptist's head in a charger" (Matthew 14:8).

Though nonbiblical sources identify the daughter of Herodias as Salome, the girl who requested John the Baptist's head on a platter is not named in scripture (Matthew 14, Mark 6).

There is a Salome in
the Bible, mentioned in
Mark 15:40 and 16:1. In
comparing Mark 15:40–41
with Matthew 27:56, some
extrapolate that she is
the wife of Zebedee and
mother of Jesus' disciples
James and John.

Job's wife has often been criticized for encouraging her suffering husband to "curse God, and die" (Job 2:9). But it should be remembered that she too had just suffered the loss of all her physical possessions and, even worse, of her ten children.

Hoglah was one of the five daughters of Zelophehad, an Israelite who died during the wilderness wandering. She and her sisters requested his land, and God granted the request. . .with the condition that the men they ultimately married would belong to their same tribe (Numbers 27).

Abigail provided food for David and his men after her husband, Nabal, disrespected them. After Abigail explained the situation to Nabal, he died suddenly. David then married Abigail (1 Samuel 25).

God used a demon-possessed servant girl to ultimately save the Philippian jailer's soul. The girl's owners used her as a fortune teller, but when Paul cast out her demon, he and Silas were accused of stirring up trouble in Philippi. Later that night, after God miraculously set them free, Paul and Silas led the jailer to faith in Christ (Acts 16:16–40).

Though she was likely not a believer, Pilate's wife had a dream warning the Roman governor that he was wrong to condemn Jesus. Pilate did not take her concerns to heart and ordered Jesus crucified (Matthew 27).

Haggith, a wife of King David, gave birth to their son, Adonijah, in Hebron (2 Samuel 3:2–4). Her name means "festive."

Jesus said that any woman who does God's will can be considered His mother or sister (Mark 3:31–35).

Abishag was a beautiful young woman chosen to provide care to the old and infirm King David. After his death, David's son Adonijah requested Abishag as his wife. King Solomon, fearing intrigue, had Adonijah executed (1 Kings 1–2).

Four Old Testament women appear in Jesus' genealogy in Matthew 1, all of them with "baggage"—Tamar, Rahab, Bathsheba, and Ruth. It seems God was demonstrating that Jesus is a savior for all people.

A woman named Claudia gained a single mention in scripture, sending her greetings to Timothy through the apostle Paul (2 Timothy 4:21).

The name of Azubah,
mother of Judah's
generally good King
Jehoshaphat (1 Kings
22:42), means "desertion"
or "forsaken."

Sarah, Abraham's wife,
lived to the age of 127
(Genesis 23:1).

King Solomon's successor,
his son Rehoboam,
had been born to an
Ammonite woman named
Naamah (1 Kings 14:21).
She was one of his seven
hundred wives and from
a pagan nation.

Bernice is a Greek name meaning "bringing victory." With her brother Herod Agrippa II, she heard the legal arguments—and the Gospel presentation—Paul made before the Judean governor Festus (Acts 24–26).

The term *Ruhamah* is a descriptor of God's mercy and compassion; however, the prefix *Lo* is a reversal. So Hosea's daughter's name, Lo-Ruhamah, was an indication of God's withdrawing of His mercy and compassion toward Israel (Hosea 1:6).

When a "sinful" woman anointed Jesus in a Pharisee's home, Jesus used her extravagant display as an example. She wet Jesus' feet with her tears, dried them with her hair, and anointed them with expensive perfume. In response to other visitors' grumbling, Jesus asked which debtor would love a forgiving creditor the most. . .the answer being "the one who had the bigger debt forgiven." Jesus said the woman, whose sins were many, was forgiven for her love and faith (Luke 7:43 NIV).

Susanna means "a white lily." She is mentioned just once in scripture, among a group of women who supported Jesus and His disciples financially (Luke 8:3).

Scripture describes Jehoaddan as the mother of Judah's King Amaziah (2 Kings 14:1). That would have made her wife of King Joash. Both her husband and her son were ultimately assassinated.

The queen of Sheba may
have visited Solomon
to discuss trade issues,
trying to impress Israel's
king with expensive gifts.
But she recognized his
incredible wisdom as a
gift from God and raved,
"Happy are these thy
servants, which stand
continually before thee,
and that hear thy wisdom"
(1 Kings 10:8).

Zebudah means "bestowal" or "a gift." This wife of King Josiah gave birth to Jehoiakim, who would rule Judah for eleven years before being deposed and killed by King Nebuchadnezzar of Babylon (2 Kings 23–24).

Rachel, Jacob's beloved wife, died giving birth to her second son, Benjamin. In her travail, she had called him Benoni ("son of my sorrow"). Jacob changed the name to "son of the right hand" (Genesis 35:16–20).

Vashti, the beautiful queen of Persia, offended her husband, King Ahasuerus, by refusing to appear at a seven-day, wine-fueled banquet for his nobles. She was removed from her position, allowing the young Jew Esther to become her replacement... and protect the Jews from an evil plot.

Zeresh was the wife of Haman, villain of the story of Esther. She, along with friends, encouraged Haman to build the gallows on which to hang Esther's cousin Mordecai (Esther 5)—the gallows that Haman himself would later die on.

The Proverbs say a virtuous woman is "a crown to her husband" (12:4).

Persis was described by the apostle Paul as "beloved" and noted as someone who had done significant work for the Lord (Romans 16:12).

The meaning of
the name *Priscilla*,
a missionary coworker
of the apostle Paul
(Romans 16:3), is "ancient"
or "venerable."

God could use even the lustful, lying wife of Potiphar for His own good purposes. When this woman falsely accused Joseph of sexual impropriety, the young Hebrew was thrown into the prison from which he would ultimately emerge as Egypt's second in command (Genesis 39–41). The Middle East would be saved from famine, and the line of God's Messiah continued.

According to Luke, "many" women supported Jesus financially as He traveled from town to town "preaching and shewing the glad tidings of the kingdom of God" (Luke 8:1–3).

The name *Julia* appears once in scripture (Romans 16:15). She was among a group of Roman believers saluted by the apostle Paul.

Both Sarah and her daughter-in-law Rebekah tried to "assist" God's plans. Impatient for the son God promised, Sarah encouraged her husband, Abraham, to have a child by her servant girl, Hagar (Genesis 16). Years later, Abraham and Sarah's promised child, Isaac, was tricked by his wife, Rebekah, into granting the family blessing to her favored son, Jacob (Genesis 27). Though God worked out His good plans anyway, each woman's impatience created trouble.

For three months,
Moses' mother, Jochebed,
disobeyed the pharaoh's
command to throw her
newborn into the Nile
River. When she could
hold out no longer,
she did put the boy in
the water. . .but in a sealed
basket. God miraculously
directed the pharaoh's
daughter to the baby,
who was adopted into
the ruler's household
(Exodus 1:22–2:10).

One of Israel's judges, Jephthah, made a rash promise to God that he would sacrifice the first thing that crossed the threshold of his home as he returned victorious from battle. To his dismay, that was his daughter—but she bravely accepted her father's promise (Judges 11).

According to the psalm writer, God can make "the barren woman to keep house, and to be a joyful mother of children" (Psalm 113:9).

Anna, a prophetess who saw the baby Jesus when He was presented in the temple, was quite elderly, either eighty-four years old or having been widowed for eighty-four years, depending on the translation (Luke 2:36–38).

Jesus had at least two sisters. His neighbors in Nazareth, taking offense at His teaching, said, "Isn't this the carpenter's son? Isn't his mother's name Mary, and aren't his brothers James, Joseph, Simon and Judas? Aren't all his sisters with us?" (Matthew 13:55–56 NIV).

The Bible mentions
two women who were
mothers of twins:
Rebekah, who birthed
Esau and Jacob to Isaac
(Genesis 25), and Tamar,
mother of Pharez and
Zarah by Judah
(Genesis 38).

Childless Hannah saw her husband's second wife bearing children and begged God for a son. He answered her prayers with Samuel, whom she returned to the Lord's service at the temple as soon as he was weaned (1 Samuel 1).

Noadiah, a prophetess who opposed Nehemiah's rebuilding of the walls of Jerusalem, appears only a single time in scripture (Nehemiah 6:14).

The name of Michaiah, mother of Judah's King Abijah (2 Chronicles 13:1–2), means "Who is like Jehovah?"

A poor widow in
Zarephath sacrificed her
last bit of food for the
prophet Elijah. . .only to
see God miraculously
multiply her flour and
oil (1 Kings 17).

In the Old Testament, God was particularly hard on anyone who took advantage of widows: "Cursed be he that perverteth the judgment of the stranger, fatherless, and widow. And all the people shall say, Amen" (Deuteronomy 27:19).

Some believe Apphia, mentioned once in scripture in Philemon 2, was Philemon's wife. The apostle Paul mentioned her immediately after greeting Philemon, calling her "our beloved."

The male lover in
the Song of Solomon
complimented his bride
by describing her teeth
as "a flock of sheep just
shorn" and her neck as
"the tower of David built
with course of stone"
(4:2, 4).

The name of Syntyche, a coworker with Paul who needed the apostle's urging to get along with another churchwoman, Euodias, may indicate "fortunate" (Philippians 4:2–3).

Samson's mother, unnamed in the Bible, was told by an angel that she would conceive and give birth to a son. She was to keep him from unclean foods, wine and strong drink, and haircuts as part of his Nazarite separation to God (Judges 13).

Michal, whose husband,
David, replaced her father,
Saul, as king, was offended
by David's exuberant
dancing as he brought the
ark of the covenant into
Jerusalem. Her attitude
toward God's anointed
king apparently made her
childless (2 Samuel 6).

Young David had earned the right to marry Saul's daughter Michal by killing two hundred Philistines, twice the number demanded by the king (1 Samuel 18).

Dinah was the daughter
of Jacob and Leah
(Genesis 46:15). Her
name means "justice"
or "one who judges."

Lydia, the first Christian convert in Europe, was a businesswoman. The King James Version calls her "a seller of purple," while the New Living Translation describes her as "a merchant of expensive purple cloth" (Acts 16:14).

The prophet Isaiah called his wife "the prophetess." We don't know her name, but her son was called Maher-Shalal-Hash-Baz (Isaiah 8:1–4)!

Delilah may have originally charmed the Jewish judge Samson. But she conquered him with "nagging" (Judges 16:16 NIV).

Ephah could indicate a unit of measurement (about a bushel), serve as a man's name (there were two), or act as a woman's name. She was a concubine of a man named Caleb (1 Chronicles 2:46).

Esther underwent a
twelve-month beauty
regimen as preparation
for her competition to
become the new queen
of Persia (Esther 2:12).

In Bible times, women were generally responsible for traveling to the local well to draw water for the family. The task was often done in the evening, with the liquid carried back in a clay jar balanced on the head or shoulder.

The oft-married Samaritan woman Jesus met at the public well was drawing water around noon (John 4)—probably because she was trying to avoid interacting with judgmental neighbors in the busier evening hours.

Surprisingly, God's name never appears in the book of Esther. But her call for fellow Jews to fast for her (Esther 4:16) implies that He was clearly working in the background.

Little is known of Eglah in the scriptures, except for her being a wife of King David and mother of his son Ithream (2 Samuel 3:5, 1 Chronicles 3:3).

Serah appears three times in scripture (Genesis 46:17, Numbers 26:46, 1 Chronicles 7:30) as a daughter of Asher and therefore a granddaughter of Jacob.

Many women must
have brushed against or
otherwise had contact
with Jesus' garments. But
scripture records only one
being healed by such a
touch (Matthew 9:19–22).
The difference? "Thy faith
hath made thee whole,"
Jesus said.

Moses' sister, Miriam, watched over her baby brother as he floated in a basket on the edge of the Nile. When Pharaoh's daughter found the crying boy, Miriam quickly asked if she could fetch a Jewish nurse for him. When the answer was yes, Miriam called on Jochebed, Moses' own mother. . .who was *paid* for her work (Exodus 2:8–10)!

Maachah, daughter of the king of Geshur, was another wife of King David. She was mother to Absalom (1 Chronicles 3:2).

Laban gave his servant girl Zilpah to his daughter Leah when she married Jacob. Caught up in the troubled family dynamic between Leah and her favored sister, Rachel, she gave birth to Jacob's sons Gad and Asher, heads of two tribes of Israel (Genesis 35:26).

Cozbi was a woman of Midian who was executed, along with her Israelite lover, to end a plague on God's people (Numbers 25).

Taphath was a daughter
of King Solomon who
married one of her father's
officials (1 Kings 4:11).
Her name indicates
"a drop of myrrh."

The witch of Endor, though breaking Saul's command by practicing witchcraft in Israel, attempted to help the hypocritical king who had come seeking her services. After Saul received notice of his imminent death from the spirit of Samuel, the woman urged Saul to eat for his strength, going so far as to kill a calf and bake bread for him (1 Samuel 28).

Though Jesus never married, the apostle Paul indicates that His brothers did (1 Corinthians 9:5).

The meaning of the name *Elisabeth* (Luke 1) is "the oath" or "fullness of God."

Elisheba, daughter of a man named Amminidab, became wife of Moses' brother Aaron. Through their union, the priestly lineage began with sons Nadab, Abihu, Eleazar, and Ithamar.

While the early church was expected to care for widows, the apostle Paul commanded that the children or grandchildren of widows should make the first provision for them (1 Timothy 5).

Ahinoam and Abigail,
wives of David before he
was crowned king, were
once taken captive by the
Amalekites. But David
attacked his enemies
and saved both women
(1 Samuel 30).

Naomi, Ruth's mother-in-law, changed her own name to *Mara*, meaning "bitter." She was bitter over the loss of her husband and two sons in a time of famine (Ruth 1:20–21).

Drusilla, mentioned once in Acts 24, was daughter of Herod Agrippa I and wife of Felix, Roman procurator of Judea. She listened in on the trial of the apostle Paul.

Mary Magdalene was the first person to encounter the risen Jesus. As she stood outside the open tomb crying, He spoke her name, then told her to inform the other disciples that He was alive (John 20).

When Jacob's daughter Dinah was defiled by Hamor, a Hivite prince, her brothers Simeon and Levi retaliated by killing every man of Hamor's city (Genesis 34).

The Israelite judge Othniel won the right to marry his niece Achsah by defeating the city of Kirjath-sepher in battle. Achsah, whose name means "anklet," was the prize offered by her father, Caleb (Joshua 15).

The apostle Paul used a variant name for his coworker Priscilla in his second letter to Timothy: Prisca (4:19).

When Jael killed the Canaanite commander Sisera by driving a tent peg through his head, she was fulfilling a prophecy of Deborah. Israel's only female judge had agreed to her military commander's request to accompany him, but she told Barak, "Because of the course you are taking, the honor will not be yours, for the Lord will deliver Sisera into the hands of a woman" (Judges 4:9 NIV).

Both Abraham and his son Isaac feared they might be killed over their beautiful wives. Sarah and Rebekah, respectively, were urged to say she was instead a sister (Genesis 12, 26).

When Abraham told Sarah to say she was his sister, that was partly true—they were half siblings. "[She is] the daughter of my father though not of my mother" (Genesis 20:12 NIV). Rules against marriage to close relatives would come later, in the time of Moses.

Joanna, a woman
who assisted Jesus and
the disciples financially
(Luke 8:3), has a name
meaning "God is gracious."

Hephzibah was wife of Judah's excellent King Hezekiah and mother of the evil Manasseh, whose fifty-five-year rule was the longest on record (2 Kings 21:1). Her name means "my delight is in her."

Esther's name appears fifty-six times in the King James Version of the Bible, in every instance in the book of Esther.

The apostle Paul
described women
as "the glory of man"
(1 Corinthians 11:7).

The male lover in the Song of Solomon complimented his bride by describing her navel as "a rounded goblet that never lacks blended wine" and her belly as "a mound of wheat encircled by lilies" (7:2 NIV).

Sarai, Rebekah,
Bathsheba, Tamar,
Abishag, Vashti, Esther,
and the daughters of
Job are all described
in scripture as
beautiful women.

The name of Hannah, mother of the Old Testament prophet and priest Samuel, can mean "gracious" or "favored."

Peninnah, a second wife of Elkanah, bullied Hannah over her childlessness. She is mentioned only twice in scripture (1 Samuel 1:2, 4).

The name *Naomi*, which appears twenty-one times in scripture, means "beautiful" or "agreeable."

Mentioned only once in scripture, the servant girl Rhoda's story is almost comical. She was so excited to see the apostle Peter, just released from prison by an angel, that she left him standing outside when she ran to tell the disciples that their prayers for Peter had been answered (Acts 12).

Magdalene, the surname of one of Jesus' female disciples, indicates a person from Magdala, a town on the western shore of the Sea of Galilee.

Paul addressed a woman named Mary in his greetings to the Romans (16:6). This woman, "who bestowed much labour on us," is the last of a half dozen Marys noted in scripture.

A woman named Naarah appears in two verses of scripture, 1 Chronicles 4:5–6. Her name means, appropriately, "a maiden."

Though four biblical men were called Michaiah, there was one woman by the name, the mother of Judah's King Abijah (2 Chronicles 13:2). The name means "who is like God?"

Jemima was the first daughter of Job after God restored his fortunes (Job 42:14). Her name means "dove."

When a woman broke a box of expensive perfume over Jesus, some people complained about the "waste of the ointment." But Jesus said she was anointing His body ahead of time for His burial, and that what she had done "shall be spoken of for a memorial of her" (Mark 14). Not surprisingly, He was right.

Dorcas, also known as Tabitha, a resident of the seaport town of Joppa, was known for her ability to sew, especially garments for the poor. When Peter heard that she had died, he prayed over her and she was raised back to life (Acts 9).

Timna was a concubine of Eliphaz, whose father was Esau (Genesis 36:12). Together, they had a son named Amalek, whose descendants would trouble Israel for generations.

Puah, along with
Shiphrah, a midwife
to the Hebrews, refused
to follow the pharaoh's
edict to kill the male
babies at birth. Because
of their courageous
obedience, God "gave
them families of their
own" (Exodus 1:21 NIV).

Huldah, an Old Testament prophetess, spoke a message of doom to sinful Judah, but offered encouragement to young King Josiah, who was grieved by what he found in the newly discovered book of Moses (2 Kings 22).

According to the
Proverbs, a gracious
woman "retaineth honor"
(11:16). . .or as the New
International Version
translates it, "gains honor."
(Proverbs 11:16)

An unnamed woman of Shunem blessed the prophet Elisha with hospitality. A childless woman with an aged husband, she was rewarded with a miraculous baby boy (2 Kings 4).

When Rebekah watered a stranger's camels, it was a specific answer to prayer—and confirmation that she was the chosen bride for Isaac (Genesis 24).

The woman who was healed by touching the hem of Jesus' garment had been ailing for twelve years. The Gospel writer Luke, himself a doctor, reported that she had "spent all her living upon physicians, neither could be healed of any" (Luke 8:43).

Zipporah was a daughter of Jethro, a priest in Midian. Moses defended her and her sisters from some antagonistic shepherds, and she later became his wife (Exodus 2).

A Sidonian princess who married King Ahab of Israel, Jezebel persecuted Israel's prophets, including Elijah. After his miraculous victory over the prophets of Baal at Mount Carmel, he fled for his life from Jezebel's threats (1 Kings 18–19).

The elderly prophetess Anna was the first Christian evangelist. Having seen the eight-day-old Jesus at the temple, she "spake of him to all them that looked for redemption in Jerusalem" (Luke 2:38).

Similar to the way *Pharaoh* was a title given to an Egyptian king, *Candace* was a title denoting an Ethiopian queen (Acts 8:27).

A woman of the tribe of Judah was named Hazelelponi (1 Chronicles 4:3). Some Jewish traditions identify her as the wife of Manoah and the mother of Samson.

Joanna is mentioned twice in the Gospel of Luke: first, as the wife of Herod's household manager Chuza and a financial supporter of Jesus; second, as one of the women who told the apostles of Jesus' resurrection (Luke 8:3, 24:10).

Deborah, Israel's only female judge, was also a musician. Judges 5 is her song commemorating the military victories of God's people.

Abital is identified as King David's wife and mother of his fifth son, Shephatiah (2 Samuel 3:4). But nothing further is mentioned of Abital.

Leah became wife
of the patriarch Jacob
through her father's
deception. Jacob preferred
her sister, Rachel, but
Leah birthed several sons,
including Judah, whose
lineage would include
Jesus Christ
(Genesis 29).

After Paul and Silas left their Philippian jail cell, they went to the home of Lydia, who they'd earlier led to faith in Jesus (Acts 16:40).

Atarah was the wife of
Jerahmeel, a man of
the tribe of Judah
(1 Chronicles 2:26). Her
name means "crown."

The name of Noadiah, prophetess in the time of Nehemiah (Nehemiah 6:14), means "one to whom the Lord revealed Himself."

Rahab was a prostitute in Jericho, but she hid the two spies Joshua had sent to investigate the city. She was rewarded with safety when the Israelites took the city (Joshua 6) . . .and ultimately appears in the genealogy of Jesus (Matthew 1).

Ruth, a non-Israelite who was faithful to her Jewish mother-in-law, Naomi, married the Israelite Boaz and became an ancestor of both King David and Jesus Christ (Ruth 1, Matthew 1).

Sarah's servant girl, Hagar, by whom Abraham fathered Ishmael (Genesis 16), appears briefly in the New Testament as well. The apostle Paul uses her as a stand-in for the law given at Mount Sinai (Galatians 4:24–26).

Bathsheba was married to Uriah, but King David had him murdered so that he could take her as his wife. Matthew's genealogy of Jesus, referring to their son Solomon, does not mention her name but says she "had been Uriah's wife" (Matthew 1:6 NIV).

The generous woman of Shunem, who built a guest room for Elisha, rushed to find the prophet after her son died of a sudden illness. Her faith was rewarded with the boy's resurrection (2 Kings 4).

Hamutal was the mother
of two kings of Judah—
Jehoahaz, who was
deposed by Pharaoh
Necho of Egypt, and
Zedekiah, who was
installed by the new
world power, Babylon
(2 Kings 23–24).

In Jesus' parable of
the ten virgins, half took
extra oil for their lamps
as they awaited the
bridegroom's arrival. Jesus
called them wise, because
"ye know neither the day
nor the hour wherein
the Son of man cometh"
(Matthew 25:13).

The Greek name
Dorcas (Acts 9:36)
means "gazelle."

Priscilla, along with her husband, Aquila, quietly instructed the powerful preacher Apollos in the deeper truths of Jesus: "They took him unto them, and expounded unto him the way of God more perfectly" (Acts 18:26).

Bilhah was a handmaid
to Rachel, the wife Jacob
loved more than her sister,
Leah. Bilhah gave birth
to Jacob's sons Dan and
Naphtali (Genesis 35:25).

A poor widow in Zarephath received two miracles through Elijah: first, her meager supply of flour and oil never ran out; second, the prophet raised her recently deceased son back to life (1 Kings 17).

Eve's failure in the garden of Eden ultimately exploded into intense grief, when her oldest child, Cain, killed his younger brother, Abel (Genesis 3–4). Eve's story ends with the birth of Seth in Genesis 4:25.

Hannah, whose inability to conceive led to much pain until God miraculously sent Samuel, ultimately gave birth to three boys and two girls (1 Samuel 2:21).

There are two Deborahs in the Old Testament. The first was a nurse of Isaac's wife Rebekah. Her name means "bee."

Leah was destined
to become the unloved
wife of Jacob by her
father Laban's treachery
(Genesis 29). Her name
means "wearied."

Jesus defended a woman "caught in the act of adultery" (John 8:4 NIV) by telling her accusers that "any one of you who is without sin" could be "the first to throw a stone at her" (verse 7 NIV). Shamed, the Pharisees and teachers of the law left quietly.

The aging King David's caregiver, Abishag, was expected to lie in bed with him to keep him warm (1 Kings 1).

Kezia was the second daughter of Job after God restored his fortunes (Job 42:14). Her name means "cassia."

Rebekah's family asked
if she wanted to leave
immediately to marry
Isaac, a second cousin
she had never seen. She
agreed and traveled to
Isaac's home with his
father Abraham's servant
(Genesis 24).

The male lover in the Song of Solomon complimented his bride by describing her eyes as "the fishpools in Heshbon" and her nose as "the tower of Lebanon which looketh toward Damascus" (7:4).

An Israelite named Shelomith married an Egyptian and gave birth to a son who would later be stoned for blaspheming the name of the Lord God (Leviticus 24:10–14).

Orpah stayed home in Moab when Naomi and Ruth traveled to Bethlehem (Ruth 1). While Ruth became an ancestor of Jesus Christ, Orpah is never heard from again in scripture.

Rachel, favored wife of Jacob and mother of Joseph and Benjamin, had previously been a shepherdess (Genesis 29).

The young virgin Mary, after receiving news that she would give birth to the Messiah, Jesus, spoke a poetic prayer that has come to be called "the Magnificat." It begins, "My soul doth magnify the Lord" (Luke 1).

The evil Queen Jezebel, who had engineered the death of an innocent man to acquire his vineyard, was ultimately thrown from an upper window, trampled by horses, and eaten by dogs (2 Kings 9).

The Bible mentions two people named Noah—the male builder of the ark and also one of the five daughters of a man named Zelophehad. They received his inheritance in the Promised Land because he had no sons. But they had to agree to marry within their tribe of Manasseh (Numbers 36:10–12).

Jesus commended a poor widow who gave a tiny offering at the temple. Rich people "cast in of their abundance," He said, "but she of her want did cast in all that she had, even all her living" (Mark 12:44).

A pair of prostitutes gave Israel's new king, Solomon, an opportunity to demonstrate his God-given wisdom. As the women argued over a live and a dead baby, Solomon called for a sword to divide the living child in half. When one woman immediately cried, "O my lord, give her the living child, and in no wise slay it," Solomon knew exactly who the mother was (1 Kings 3).

Hannah's intense, silent praying for a child brought judgment on her from the priest Eli, who accused her of drunkenness at the worship center. When she explained her sorrow, he relented, saying, "May the God of Israel grant you what you have asked of him" (1 Samuel 1:17).

When Rachel died, Jacob erected a pillar over the grave of his beloved wife (Genesis 35:20).

The meaning of the name *Phoebe*, described as a deacon or servant of the church in Cenchreae (Romans 16:1 NIV), is "shining" or "pure."

The name of Isaac's wife, *Rebekah*, implies a fetter or snare in Hebrew. The Greek form, *Rebecca*, is used once in the King James New Testament (Romans 9:10).

Moses' mother first appears in Exodus 2, but she is not named until Exodus 6:20: "And Amram took him Jochebed his father's sister to wife; and she bare him Aaron and Moses."

Athaliah, the only ruling queen of Judah, gained her position by killing off any potential claimants to the throne. The author of 2 Chronicles, in reporting her history (chapter 23), provided no summary like that of the other rulers of Judah. . .implying that her reign was invalid.

The name of Huldah, the prophetess who guided young King Josiah after he found the lost law of Moses, means "weasel."

Damaris, a woman of Athens, heard the apostle Paul's philosophical presentation to the Areopagus and believed in Jesus (Acts 17).

The name *Tamar*, used by three Old Testament women, means "a palm tree."

King David's handsome son Absalom was closely connected to two of the Bible's Tamars. One was his sister, and one was his daughter (2 Samuel 13:1, 14:27).

Anna, the old prophetess who welcomed baby Jesus in the temple, was from the tribe of Asher (Luke 2:36). Asher was the son of Jacob and Leah's servant Zilpah.

Zeresh, wife of Haman, the villain of the story of Esther, apparently had ten children (Esther 9:7–10).

Ruth essentially
proposed marriage
to Boaz (Ruth 3)!

After the judge Jephthah's foolish vow, the young women of Israel had a custom of lamenting his daughter four days each year (Judges 11:39–40).

The name of Elisabeth,
relative of Mary and
mother of John the
Baptist, means
"the oath of God."

Adah is the second woman mentioned by name in the Bible. Her son, Jubal, is credited as the one who introduced the art of music to the world (Genesis 4:19–21).

Delilah, who discovered
the secret of Samson's
strength and turned
him over to the enemy
Philistines, is named
six times in scripture.
Her name means
"languishing."

Mary of Bethany listened at Jesus' feet while her sister became uptight carrying out household tasks. Jesus told Martha that only one thing was "needful" and that Mary had chosen well (Luke 10).

Keturah, the name of Abraham's second wife, means "incense" or "perfumed."

The meaning of the name *Judith* (Genesis 26:34) is "Jewess" or "praised." She was a wife of Esau.

Milcah was one of Zelophehad's five daughters who received her father's inheritance in the Promised Land because he had no sons. God granted the women's request but required each to marry within their tribe, Manasseh (Numbers 36).

The name *Rachel*
means "ewe."

Sarah, Esther, and Rachel are the most mentioned women in scripture. In the King James Version, in all forms of their names, they are noted sixty-one, fifty-seven, and forty-eight times, respectively.

Moses' wife Zipporah
apparently saved his
life by circumcising
one of their sons
(Exodus 4:24–26).

Peter's raising of Dorcas (also called Tabitha) from the dead caused many people in Joppa to turn to Jesus (Acts 9).

The apostle Paul's advice for avoiding fornication: "Let every man have his own wife, and let every woman have her own husband" (1 Corinthians 7:2).

Keren-Happuch was the youngest of Job's three daughters born after God restored the suffering man's fortunes. Her name means "horn of cosmetic."

Scripture never expressly describes the church—all the true believers in Jesus—as "the bride of Christ." But that phrasing has been extrapolated from verses that describe Jesus as the bridegroom (for example, Mark 2:19–20, John 3:29).

Old Testament law
commanded a man
to marry his dead
brother's widow to
maintain the family line
(Deuteronomy 25:5–6).

The marriage rule from Deuteronomy 25 was what the Sadducees used to try to trip up Jesus with a story about a woman whose husband died, followed by all six of his brothers who married her in succession (Luke 20:27–40). Jesus' response indicated that there is no marriage in heaven.

Lydia, the businesswoman converted to Christ in Acts 16, shares a name with an Old Testament land mentioned in Jeremiah 46 and Ezekiel 30. This province of Asia Minor was known for its archers.

Zeruiah, a sister of King David, is mentioned in the Bible twenty-five times. Her three sons, Abishai, Joab, and Asahel, are named, but her husband is not.

Zilpah was Leah's maid
and mother of Jacob's sons
Gad and Asher (Genesis
35:26). Her name
means "a trickling."

Bilhah was Rachel's maid and mother of Jacob's sons Dan and Naphtali (Genesis 35:25). Her name means "timid" or "bashful."

Keturah was Abraham's concubine and second wife. Her children with Abraham included Midian, whose descendants would be enemies of the Israelites (1 Chronicles 1:32).

Ruth's gleaning in the field of Boaz was something that God's law encouraged: "And when ye reap the harvest of your land, thou shalt not wholly reap the corners of thy field, neither shalt thou gather the gleanings of thy harvest. And thou shalt not glean thy vineyard, neither shalt thou gather every grape of thy vineyard; thou shalt leave them for the poor and stranger: I am the LORD your God" (Leviticus 19:9–10).

King David had a wife
named Abigail (the widow
of the churlish Nabal) and
also a sister by that name
(1 Chronicles 2:13–16).

Outside of the Song of Solomon, the only apparently romantic kiss in scripture occurs when Jacob first meets Rachel (Genesis 29:11).

Ahinoam was the wife of Saul, anointed as Israel's first king. She was the mother of Jonathan, a dear friend of David, who would ultimately replace Saul as king (1 Samuel 14:49–50).

Mahlah was one of the
five daughters of a man
named Zelophehad, who
had no sons. The sisters
requested his inheritance
in the Promised Land
and God, through Moses,
agreed (Numbers 36).

Milcah, the wife of Abraham's brother Nahor, bore him eight children. She was also the grandmother of Rebekah (Genesis 22:20–23).

Abiah was a name used
by both men and at least
one woman of Bible times
(1 Chronicles 2:24).
It means "Jehovah
is my Father."

The appointment of the first deacons in the early church occurred because certain widows were being overlooked during the distribution of charity (Acts 6:1–7).

Meshullemeth was the wife of Judah's evil King Manasseh and mother of the equally evil King Amon (2 Kings 21:18–20). Her name means "friend."

The meaning of the name *Jochebed*, mother of Moses, Aaron, and Miriam, is "glorious" or "honorable."

Esther and Mordecai, heroes of the book of Esther, were cousins. Mordecai had raised Esther since "she had neither father nor mother" (Esther 2:7).

Basmath was a daughter of King Solomon (1 Kings 4:15). Her name means "fragrant" or "perfumed."

Rahab, the prostitute of Jericho, protected the Israelite spies because she knew "that the LORD has given you this land, and that a great fear of you has fallen on us" (Joshua 2:9 NIV). She and her family were spared when the city was overrun.

The name *Sherah* means "a female relation by blood." She was a daughter of Ephraim and is credited with building three towns (1 Chronicles 7:24).

Helah was one of two
wives of a man named
Ashur (1 Chronicles 4:5, 7).
Her name means "rust."

The name *Bithiah*
(1 Chronicles 4:18) means
"a daughter of Jehovah."

Jerusha was the wife of King Uzziah, a generally good king of Judah who ultimately contracted leprosy for intruding on the priest's duties. Her name means "married."

Rizpah, a concubine of King Saul, saw two sons killed in retaliation for Saul's behavior. Then she spent days outdoors protecting their bodies from birds and wild animals (2 Samuel 21).

The first hint of Jesus'
life and work was spoken
to Eve in the garden of
Eden: "And I will put
enmity between you and
the woman, and between
your offspring and hers he
will crush your head, and
you will strike his heel"
(Genesis 3:15 NIV).

Tahpenes was queen of Egypt during the time of Solomon. God used her brother-in-law, Hadad of Edom, to punish Solomon for his sin of false worship (1 Kings 11).

Eunice, a Jewish woman, had a son named Timothy with a Greek man. She taught Timothy to love the Lord, and he ultimately became the apostle Paul's "son in the faith" (1 Timothy 1:2).

Bathsheba, who became David's wife after his adulterous pursuit of her, had been married to Uriah, one of the thirty mightiest men in the king's army (1 Chronicles 11).

The widow of a prophet, deeply in debt due to her husband's death, enjoyed the miraculous provision of God through Elisha. He told her to borrow as many bottles and jugs as she could from neighbors, then fill them with the one pot of oil she had in her home. The oil never ran out until she had filled the final borrowed vessel (2 Kings 4).

God said His feelings toward His people are greater even than that of a woman toward her baby. "Can a mother forget the baby at her breast and have no compassion on the child she has borne? Though she may forget, may I not forget you" (Isaiah 49:15 NIV).

The name of Jehosheba, who protected the royal baby Joash from his murdering grandmother Athaliah, means "Jehovah is her oath."

Moses' sister Miriam was not only a prophetess but also a musician. When Moses composed a song commemorating the Israelites' escape through the Red Sea, Miriam accompanied it with a timbrel, or tambourine (Exodus 15).

An unnamed woman of Thebez, hiding in the city tower for protection, dropped a millstone on the head of the murderous Abimelech, a son of Gideon who had killed his seventy brothers. His injury, though serious, was not immediately fatal, and Abimelech ordered his armor bearer to end his life so it could not be said that "a woman killed him" (Judges 9:54 NIV).

Though we don't know
her name, Acts 23:16
indicates that the
apostle Paul had a sister.

Ruth's behavior after settling in Bethlehem with her mother-in-law, Naomi, was so good that Boaz stated, "All the city of my people doth know that thou art a virtuous woman" (Ruth 3:11).

A wife of King Saul and a wife of King David were each named Ahinoam, meaning "gracious."